D0196162

岸本斉史

y morning always begins with a cup coffee...

...which sounds hardboiled, but really I can only drink it if it's not black because that's too bitter.

I like it sweet. And since I've got a kid's tongue, I add a ton of milk and sugar. I want to become an adult and appreciate black coffee, but I feel like I'll never get there! Because it's so, so bitter! It's just a bitter sap!

—*Masashi Kishimoto, 2009*

Author/artist Masashi Kishimoto was born in 1974 in rural Okayama Prefecture, Japan. After spending time in art college, he won the Hop Step Award for new manga artists with his manga **Karakuri** (Mechanism). Kishimoto decided to base his next story on traditional Japanese culture. His first version of **Naruto**, drawn in 1997, was a one-shot story about fox spirits; his final version, which debuted in **Weekly Shonen Jump** in 1999, quickly became the most popular ninja manga in Japan.

NARUTO VOL. 45
SHONEN JUMP Manga Edition
This graphic novel contains material that was originally published in English in SHONEN JUMP #77. Artwork in the magazine may have been slightly altered from that presented here.

STORY AND ART BY MASASHI KISHIMOTO

Translation/Mari Morimoto
Series Touch-up Art & Lettering/Annaliese Christman
Additional Touch-up Art & Lettering/Sabrina Heep, Inori Fukuda Trant
Design/Sean Lee
Series Editor/Joel Enos
Graphic Novel Editor/Megan Bates

NARUTO © 1999 by Masashi Kishimoto. All rights reserved. First published in Japan in 1999 by SHUEISHA Inc., Tokyo. English translation rights arranged by SHUEISHA Inc.

The stories, characters and incidents mentioned in this publication are entirely fictional.

No portion of this book may be reproduced or transmitted in any form or by any means without written permission from the copyright holders.

Printed in the U.S.A.

Published by VIZ Media, LLC
P.O. Box 77010
San Francisco, CA 94107

10 9 8 7 6 5 4
First printing, July 2009
Fourth printing, August 2016

www.viz.com

PARENTAL ADVISORY
NARUTO is rated T for Teen and is recommended for ages 13 and up. This volume contains realistic and fantasy violence.

ratings.viz.com

www.shonenjump.com

SHONEN JUMP MANGA EDITION

NARUTO

VOL. 45

BATTLEFIELD, KONOHA

STORY AND ART BY

MASASHI KISHIMOTO

CHARACTERS

Naruto ナルト

Sasuke サスケ

Kakashi カカシ

Sakura サクラ

Sai サイ

Yamato ヤマト

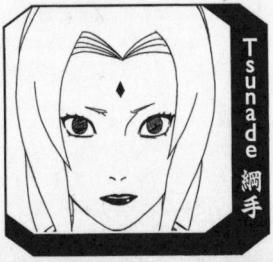
Tsunade 綱手

Jiraiya 自来也

THE STORY SO FAR...

Naruto, the biggest troublemaker at the Ninja Academy in Konohagakure, finally becomes a ninja along with his classmates Sasuke and Sakura. They grow and mature through countless trials and battles. However, Sasuke, unable to give up his quest for vengeance, leaves Konohagakure to seek Orochimaru and his power...

Two years pass. Naruto and his comrades grow up and head out once more. As their fierce battles against the Tailed Beast-targeting Akatsuki rage on, Sasuke rebels against Orochimaru and eventually absorbs him completely! Sasuke then gathers new companions and chases after his brother Itachi.

But the Uchiha brother confrontation has an unexpected result. Sasuke learns a secret about Itachi that causes him to swear vengeance...on Konoha! To start his quest, he allies with the enemies of the Leaf Ninja, the Akatsuki, and sets out to capture the Eight-Tailed Beast!

NARUTO

VOL. 45
BATTLEFIELD, KONOHA

CONTENTS

NUMBER 413: CRUMBLING 7

NUMBER 414: RAGING BULL 25

NUMBER 415: NEW POWERS!! 43

NUMBER 416: TALES OF A GUTSY SHINOBI 61

NUMBER 417: RAIKAGE ON THE MOVE!! 79

NUMBER 418: SAGE NARUTO!! 97

NUMBER 419: RAID!! 115

NUMBER 420: BATTLEFIELD, KONOHA!! 132

NUMBER 421: RECALL NARUTO!! 155

NUMBER 422: KAKASHI VS. PAIN!! 173

WHEEEEEE!!!
FW
ISH
G-
GGLOP
GLOP
Number 413: Crumbling
G-
G-GGLO
鉄
GLOP
GLOPGLOP

GLOP GLOP GLOP
LARIAT!!!!
OOSH

READ THIS WAY
HERE IT COMES...!
IT'S JUST LIKE... THAT DAY...
FSH

FWI
ISH
TMP
TMP
HE'S THE FIRST TO DODGE MY EIGHT TAILS FORM SINCE BROTHER!

READ THIS WAY
VWEENT...
SHOOSH
AIEE!
HE'S GOING AFTER THE OTHERS!
YO, FIRST I'LL SQUASH Y'ALL FLAT, SPLAT-SPLAT ♪
ZWOO
VWOO

KA
BOO
TAK
UGH...
SPLOOSH
SPLOOSH
UNH...
THUD
BOOM
THUD
SPLOOSH
SPLOOS
GAH!
THOK
SPLOO

KAROOMB-KAROOMB-KAROOMB
(STORM CLOUD RAVINE)
UGH...
SPLISH
ARE YOU ALL RIGHT?!
YEAH...
BAROOMB
...HE ONLY MOVES IN A LINEAR FASHION... SO WITH THE SHARINGAN, I SHOULD BE ABLE TO SEE HIM COMING...
ALTHOUGH HE'S DEFINITELY GOT SPEED AND POWER...
TMP
VO
OSH
IF YOU REALLY THINK YOU CAN STAY AHEAD !!
I NEED YOU TO RELAY HIS LOCATION TO US AT ALL TIMES!
KARIN! READ HIS CHAKRA AND ANTICIPATE HIS MOVEMENTS!

SASUKE !!

PH
OO
M
... GENJUTSU, HUH...
THOSE EYES... THE SHARIN-GAN...
FZMP
WOO
MPH
CAN'T MOVE...
FROM
HUF
HUF
FWITT

DRIAN

SHOOM
WHEEEEEEE!!
FSH
FWI
TAP
SKRITCH
!
UGH...
SHOOM
TMP

HE'S HURT REALLY BAD.
HUF
HUF

HE IS LIKE MY REINCAR-NATION.

...

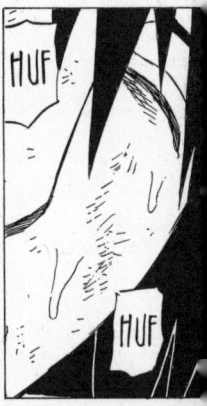
HUF
HUF

FRRLLP

SSH
ZZWOO

SINCE HIS BODY WAS COMPATIBLE WITH MY CURSE MARK, IT SHOULD WORK...
I'M GOING TO MERGE WITH HIM.
ZWOOO...

BESIDES, YOU DON'T HAVE ENOUGH CHAKRA RIGHT NOW, DO YOU?
KARIN, DON'T WORRY... I'LL DO IT THIS TIME.
HOW?

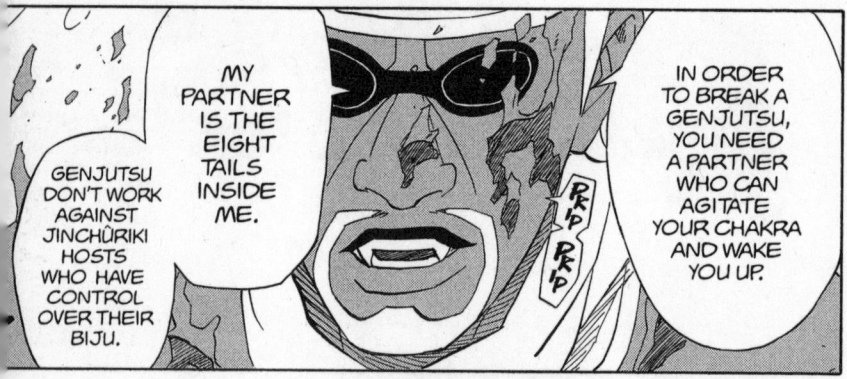
GENJUTSU DON'T WORK AGAINST JINCHŪRIKI HOSTS WHO HAVE CONTROL OVER THEIR BIJU.
MY PARTNER IS THE EIGHT TAILS INSIDE ME.
IN ORDER TO BREAK A GENJUTSU, YOU NEED A PARTNER WHO CAN AGITATE YOUR CHAKRA AND WAKE YOU UP.
RK'P
RK'P

HOST TRANS-FORMATION, YO ♪
...IS THAT OF A MONSTA', SEE I TOLD YA ♪

ZWOOO
MY TRUE MODE AS THE BIJU'S ABODE ...
YOUR ILLUSIONS I OBLITERATE, THEN Y'ALL I SHALL ANNIHILATE ♪

!

OOOSH
NOW LOOK UPON ME AS I MAKE YA PEE ALL IN YOUR PANTS, YA LIL' ANTS ♪

VIW
...

Number 414: Raging Bull
SUCH CHAKRA... CAN'T BE... NO WAY...
THOMP
A MONSTER OX...
...SO THIS IS HIS TRUE FORM, EH...

TO SPEAR MY FOES I WAS BORN ♪
...A GLORIOUS LONG-HORN ♪
WHEEEEEE!!!

ZWOOO...

JUGO, ARE YOU DONE YET?!
HIS CHAKRA IS OFF THE CHARTS. WE CAN'T STAY HERE... WE'LL BE KILLED!!

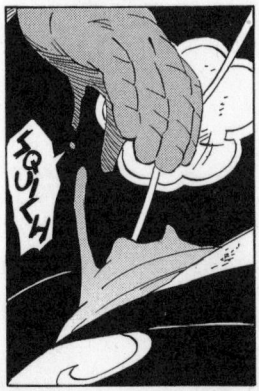
KSUKH

OH, PHEW, HE'S ALIVE. ♡
BACK WITH US, SASUKE ?!
C'MON, HURRY AND WAKE UP!

UNH...

HNNFF
HUF
HUF
HUF
HUF
HNNFF

?!
HUH?!! HE'S TURNED INTO A CHILD... WHY?

JUGO ...
I WON'T LET YOU DIE...
CUZ YOU'RE A MEMENTO OF KIMIMARO.
HUF
HUF
HNFF

HUF
HUF
SHUP
COME ON! HURRY!
WE GOTTA RUN!!

WHEEEEEE!!!

OOSH
OOSH
!!
NO ....!
FWOO
SO YOU ARE A WATER-STYLE SHINOBI...
...AND YOU HAVE THE ADVANTAGE OF THE TERRAIN.
I'VE GOT IT HERE.
RUN WHILE YOU CAN!
KERPLOOSH

READ THIS WAY
ZW
YO, I'M NOT LETTING Y'ALL GET AWAY THIS LATE IN THE GAME, FOOLS, YA FOOLS!
SUIGETSU ...
FWOP
LET'S GO, SASUKE!
HUF
HUF
HEH... I CAN'T BELIEVE...
I'VE VOLUNTEERED MY OWN BODY TO COVER THEM, SO MANY TIMES...
VWEEN
ZWOOOOOOOOSH
TAK

RRA
ARA
TH-THAT REALLY DOESN'T LOOK GOOD!!
SHOOM
WOOOOO
FOOSH
AARGH!!

KABOOM
OOOOOM

I CAN SEE IT!!

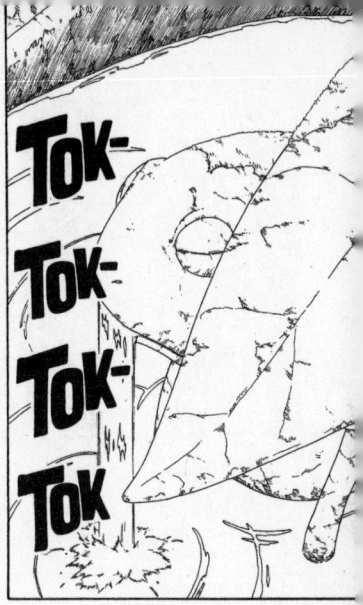
TOK-
TOK-
TOK-
TOK

NARUTO-BOY, TIME TA TAKE A BREAK. LET'S GO EAT.
WOOHOO! WOOHOO!

IT SEEMS HE'S FINALLY STARTIN' TA BE ABLE TA SENSE NATURE ENERGY.

FSSSH
FSSSH

Y...
YESSIR !!

EAT UP, BOY! ONCE YER BREAK IS OVER, YER GONNA TRY LIFTIN' ONE OF THOSE STONE FROGS USIN' SAGE JUTSU.
HARRUMP
HARRUMP
...

ULP...
NOW, WE'LL EVENTUALLY GET TA THE REAL EXERCISE...
...BUT FIRST, WHY DON'T YA TRY LIFTIN' ONE USIN' YER NIN-JUTSU CHAKRA ALONE.

SHKUK
RIGHT-O!

O-OK...
FSH

ALL RIGHT, STOP!!
GRRR RRRRR !! WON'T BUDGE ...!!!
SHKKK

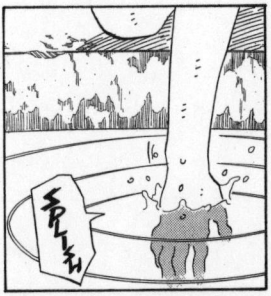
SPLASH

SURE!
SHUP

HUF
HUF
NOW TRY MIXIN' UP SOME SAGE JUTSU CHAKRA!

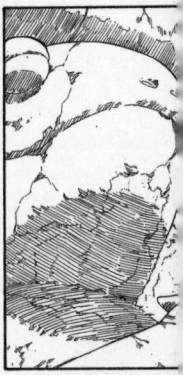

READ THIS WAY
SHK
EEN
GRRR RRRR RRRR!!
SHK UK
SURE !!
GOOD! NOW TRY LIFTIN' THIS HERE STONE FROG AGAIN!

THIS LAD'S QUICKER ON THE UPTAKE THAN JIRAIYA-BOY!
GLOP
NICE, NARUTO!
THOOM
YAH!!
THOUGH HE'S A LOT DENSER THAN JIRAIYA-BOY, TOO...
FOOL! DON'T LET IT KEEL OVER!
HOW DARE YOU DO SUCH A THING TO YOUR PREDE-CESSOR!
SPROINK
SPROINK
SHWOO!
I DID IT! I LIFTED IT UP!

READ THIS WAY
WH-WHAT IS IT, PARTNER ?!
DON'T TELL ME THAT'S LORD KILLER BEE'S...
RRRRRUMBLE
SHOOM SHOOM
COME!
TAK
YES-SIR!
TH-THAT'S ...!
!!

THE ONES WHO TOOK YUGITO AWAY...
!
THOSE ROBES... ARE THEY AKATSUKI?

AND AFTER ALL THAT LECTURING FROM LORD RAIKAGE!
LORD KILLER BEE... WHY HAS HE TRANS-FORMED INTO EIGHT TAILS?!
SIR, LOOK BELOW!
HE'S BATTLING SOMEONE!

READ THIS WAY
WE'RE NOT GOING TO BE ABLE TO GET AWAY... SO WHAT NOW?!
I CAN'T BELIEVE SUIGETSU IS ALL MESSED UP... GAH!
HUF
HUF
HUF
HUF
HUF
HUF
HUF
HUF

CUZ YOU'RE A MEMENTO OF KIMIMARO.
I WON'T LET YOU DIE...

HERE! HURRY UP AND BITE ME, SASUKE!

...

I'VE GOT IT HERE.
RUN WHILE YOU CAN!

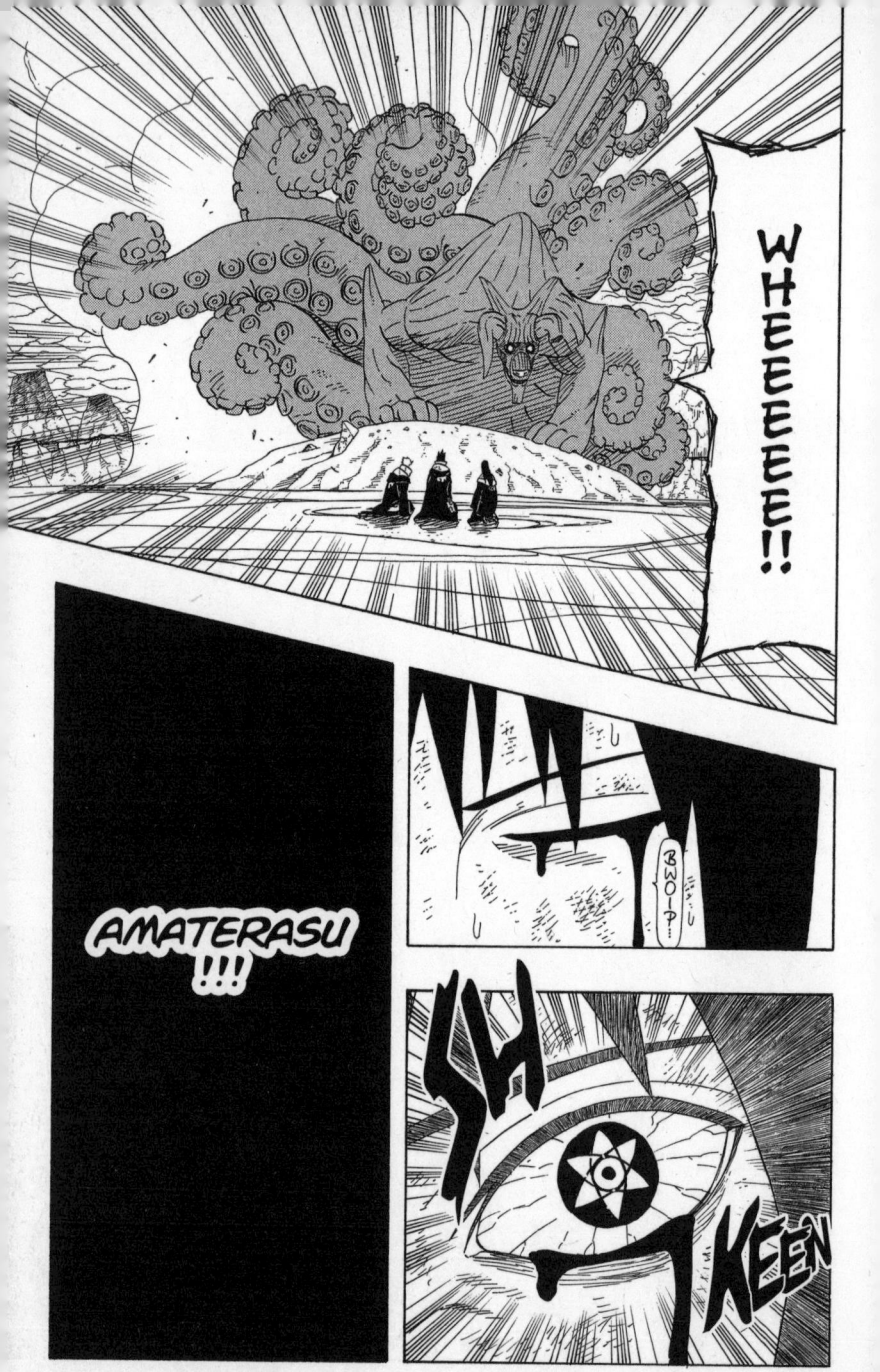
WHEEEEE!!
BWOIP...
AMATERASU !!!
SH
KEEN

NARUTO

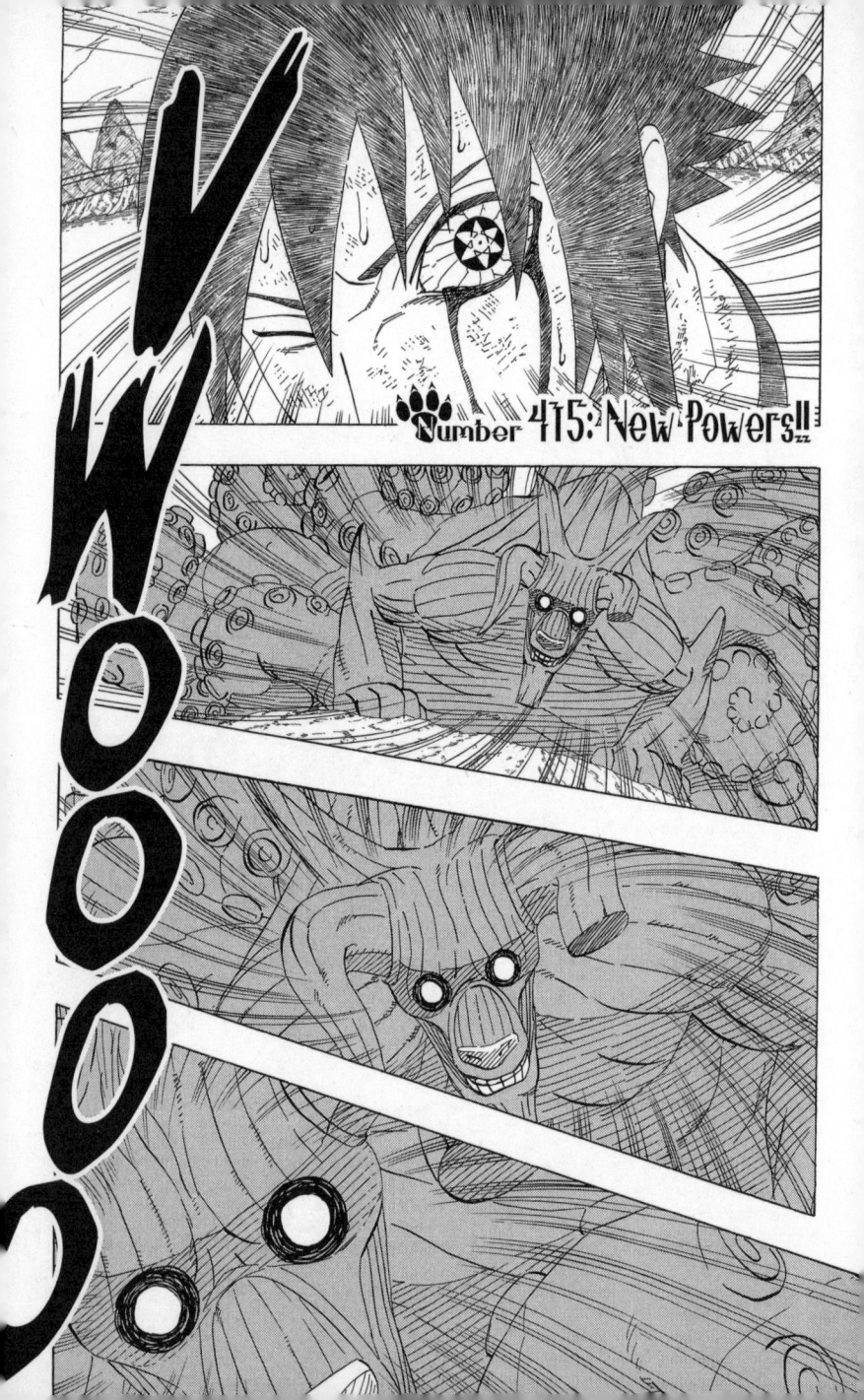
Number 415: New Powers!!

Number 415: New Powers!!

AAARGH!!
FA
BO
D
D
FA
BOOSH
WH-
WHOA
...!

SPLOOSH
AAARGH!!
YAAARGH!
SPRRSHH
TOK
UGH!
GAH!
TAK
SWOOSH
!

READ THIS WAY
SPLAAAT
AIEE!
SPLAT
SPLAT
SPLOOSH
TAK
FWTAP
HUUUOO
!
SRFSSFH

!
ZZZLE
ZZZLE
!
HUF
HUF
GLUB-
GLUB-
GLUB-
GLUB
GLUB
AIEE!
BWHAM
KARIN, RUN!
SPLAT
SPLOOSH
TOK

FABOOOSHH
WAIT, JUGO!
FTOK
NO!
...KARIN'S A GONER! WE NEED TO GET AWAY BEFORE WE GET CAUGHT TOO!!
GAH! SHE'S ON FIRE!!
KARIN!
ZWUP
FSH
FIZZLE...
ZWOO...

TOK
FWISS...
WHAT ...?
I PUT IT OUT...!
SHIKI
AAARGH!!
!
NOO
HURRY!
JUGO! GRAB KARIN!
!

VWOOOOO
AAARGH!!
FABOOOOSHH
FWAP
FWOP
HOW'S THAT POSSIBLE, SASUKE?
THE BLACK FLAMES... EXTIN-GUISHED.
THOMP

HUF
IS THIS ANOTHER POWER OF THE MANGEKYO?!
HUF

...THE BLACK FLAMES OF AMATE-RASU...
I WAS ABLE TO EXTIN-GUISH...
HUF
HUF

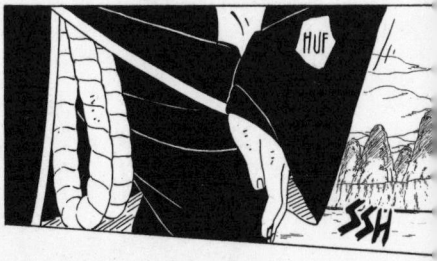
HUF
SSH

AAARGH ...

FABOOOSHH
IN WHICH CASE...

READ THIS WAY
FSSHHH-FSSHHH-FSSH
SHKEN
UGH...
FWISS
UNH...
OKAY, LET'S GRAB HIM AND GO.
THEN... WE DID MANAGE TO TAKE HIM DOWN WITHOUT KILLING HIM...
리르리는 리르리는
EIGHT TAILS... HE'S STILL ALIVE.
...BUT JUST BARELY.

WHO AND WHAT ARE THEY?!
IT CAN'T BE...
DON'T TELL ME LORD KILLER BEE'S BEEN TAKEN DOWN...?

THAT'S AN UCHIHA CREST!

WHAT IS IT, SIR?
WAIT A MINUTE!

THEY'RE AKATSUKI. QUITE FEARSOME OPPONENTS FOR SURE, BUT...

HE IS NOT GOING TO BE PLEASED...
...WHEN HE FINDS OUT HIS YOUNGER BROTHER HAS BEEN CAPTURED...

UCHIHA?
RATHER THAN TRYING TO INTERFERE, IT WOULD BE BEST FOR US TO REPORT THIS TO LORD RAIKAGE RIGHT AWAY.

...THOUGH I REALLY DIDN'T EXPECT WE'D HAVE SUCH A FIGHT ON OUR HANDS.
YEAH...
SHUP

YOU SEEM QUITE AFFECTED, PHYSICALLY.
ESPECIALLY SINCE IN ADDITION TO NO LONGER HAVING OROCHIMARU'S CURSE MARK ...
...YOU HAVEN'T QUITE HEALED FROM YOUR BATTLE AGAINST ITACHI.

BUT NOW...

IT APPEARS YA'VE MASTERED TOAD OIL-ASSISTED CONTROL.

TOK-TOK-TOK-TOK

NOW YA NEED TO MASTER CONTROLLIN' NATURE ENERGY WITHOUT USIN' TOAD OIL.

SPRRSHH

...

I CAN FEEL THE POWER FLOWING INTO ME!
TMP

TOK
TOK
TOK

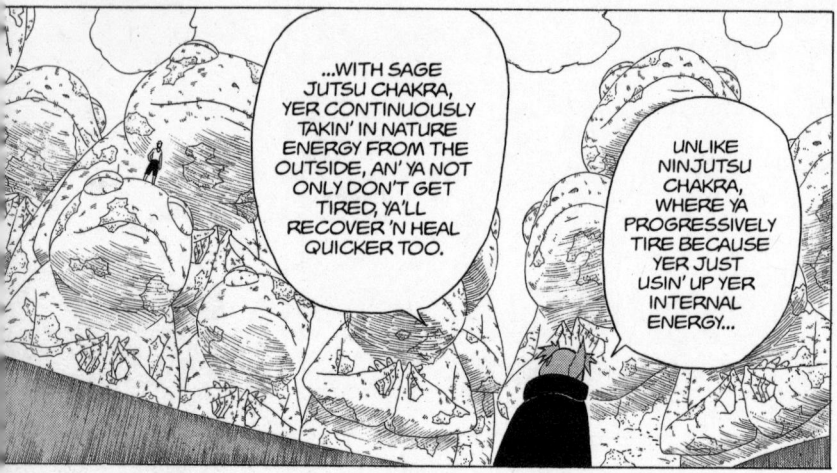
...WITH SAGE JUTSU CHAKRA, YER CONTINUOUSLY TAKIN' IN NATURE ENERGY FROM THE OUTSIDE, AN' YA NOT ONLY DON'T GET TIRED, YA'LL RECOVER 'N HEAL QUICKER TOO.
UNLIKE NINJUTSU CHAKRA, WHERE YA PROGRESSIVELY TIRE BECAUSE YER JUST USIN' UP YER INTERNAL ENERGY...

NOW MAYBE I CAN DO THAT TOO...

HUH...

WELL... WITH NINE TAILS' CHAKRA IN THE MIX TOO, HE'S SHOWIN' A TRULY OUTLANDISH RECOVERY RATE...

OH! NO, NO!
IT'S NOTH-ING!
!
EH?!

WHAT?

WHAT'S THAT?
TMP
A BOOK.

I THOUGHT I'D GIVE YA THIS TODAY, NARUTO-BOY.
NEVER MIND, THEN... BUT HERE.
FSH

A LOT OF JIRAIYA-BOY'S MIND 'N HEART ARE CONTAINED WITHIN...
IT'S JIRAIYA-BOY'S FIRST NOVEL.

A BOOK?
SSH

YA OUGHTA READ IT.

...

TALES OF A GUTSY SHINOBI

TALES... OF A GUTSY.. SHINOBI...

NARUTO

Number 416: Tales of a Gutsy Shinobi

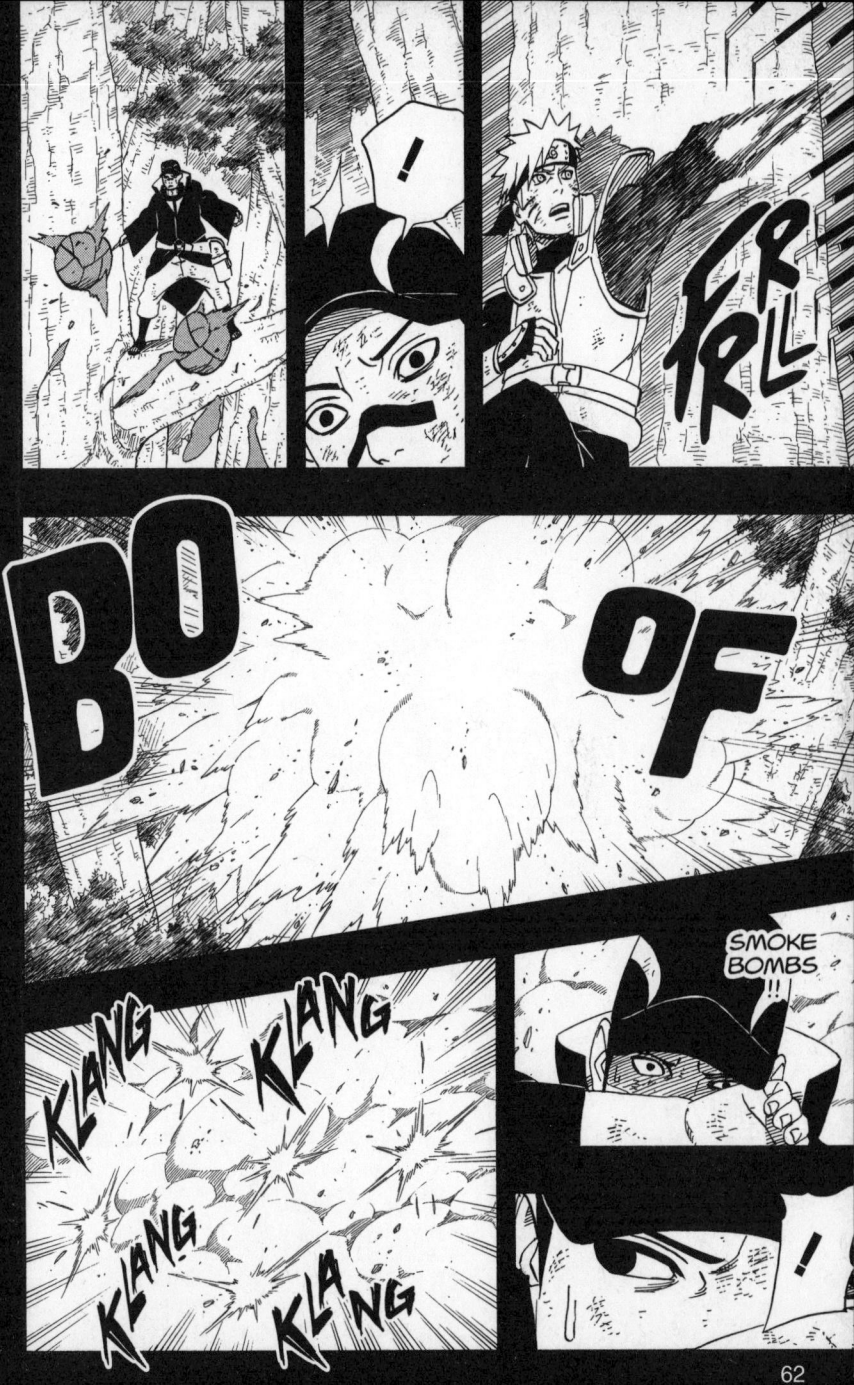
!
FR
FR
LL
BO
OF
SMOKE BOMBS !!
KLANG
KLANG
KLANG
KLANG
!

READ THIS WAY
ARGH!
HUF
HUF
I JUST HAVE ONE THING TO SAY ...
SURREN-DER.
I'M NOT INTERESTED IN HEARING IT... GIVE UP ALREADY!!
DWHAM
THWACK

BOOF
?!
GIVE UP...
!
...TRYING TO MAKE ME GIVE UP.
SHNN TOK
A SHADOW DOPPEL-GANGER!
!
THOK
WHACK

READ THIS WAY
...
AS LONG AS WE LIVE IN THIS CURSED SHINOBI WORLD... THERE WILL NEVER BE PEACE...
HEH HEH HEH ...
...E-EVEN IF YOU TAKE ME OUT, ANOTHER ASSASSIN WILL JUST COME TO ATTACK YOUR VILLAGE ...
UGH...
IF THERE'S SUCH A THING AS PEACE, I'LL FIND IT!
I'M NOT GIVING UP.
...I'LL BREAK THE CURSE.
IN THAT CASE ...
MY NAME IS...
FSH
WH-WHO ARE YOU ...?
...

SNF
SNF...
TALES OF A GUTSY SHINOBI

FKKL LP

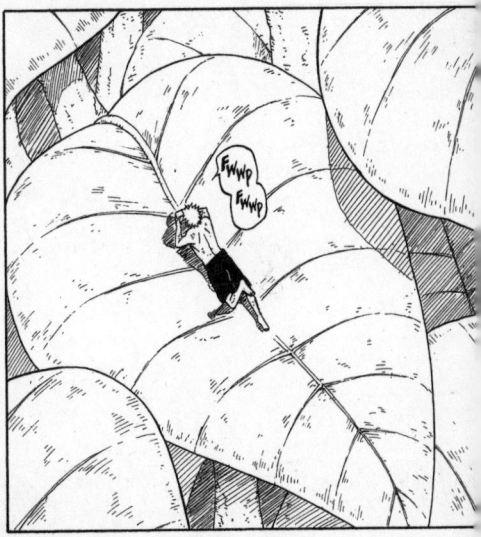
FWWP
FWWP

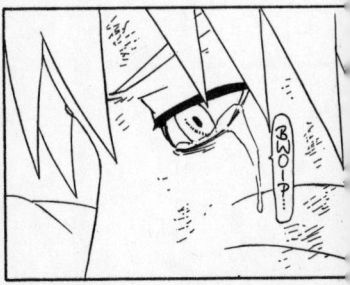
SWO-P...

READ THIS WAY
...
...AND THAT I COULD NEVER UNDERSTAND HIS FEELINGS...
SASUKE SAID HE WAS GOING TO SEVER HIS BOND WITH ME AND BECOME STRONGER ...
THAT'S WHEN HE BECAME OBSESSED WITH FORBIDDEN JUTSU.
OROCHIMARU WENT LOONY AFTER HIS PARENTS WERE KILLED.
SO WHY DID OROCHIMARU DESERT THE VILLAGE ...
...AND DECIDE TO DESTROY KONOHA?
YOU WERE FRIENDS WITH OROCHIMARU WAY BACK, RIGHT, PERVY SAGE?
...PERHAPS HE WAS RIGHT, AND I DIDN'T...
I'M LIKE YOU...
...HE YELLED AT ME THAT I DIDN'T UNDERSTAND ANYTHING ...
MY PARENTS WEREN'T KILLED, SO...
...I DON'T KNOW IF HE WAS TRYING TO RESURRECT HIS PARENTS OR WREAK VENGEANCE ON THE VILLAGE RESPONSIBLE FOR THEIR DEATHS.

...EVEN I CAN SEE THERE'S TOO MUCH HATE IN OUR SHINOBI WORLD...
BUT...
...
油
...BUT I'M NOT SURE HOW TO GO ABOUT IT YET...
I'M ALWAYS THINKING THAT I WANT TO DO SOMETHING ABOUT THIS HATRED...
HATE ...?
WOW, THAT'S KINDA DEEP.
...THAT EVENTUALLY THE DAY WILL COME WHEN ALL PEOPLE WILL UNDERSTAND ONE ANOTHER AND LIVE IN HARMONY!!
BUT I TRULY BELIEVE ...

SWSH
YES-SIR!!
CAN'T REFUSE YOUR ORDERS, PERVY SAGE!
WELL THEN, IF I CAN'T FIND THE SOLUTION MYSELF, SHALL I PASS THE QUEST ON TO YOU?!
I FEEL REDEEMED BY YOUR SMILING FACE.
HUH?
WHAT'S SO FUNNY?!
NWA-HA HA HA!!
R-REALLY?!
I'M GLAD I MADE YOU MY STUDENT!
HEH HEH...

NOTEBOOK
?
I PLAN TO CHANGE THIS WORLD WITH MY BOOKS!

BUT I HAVEN'T GIVEN UP YET, YOU KNOW!

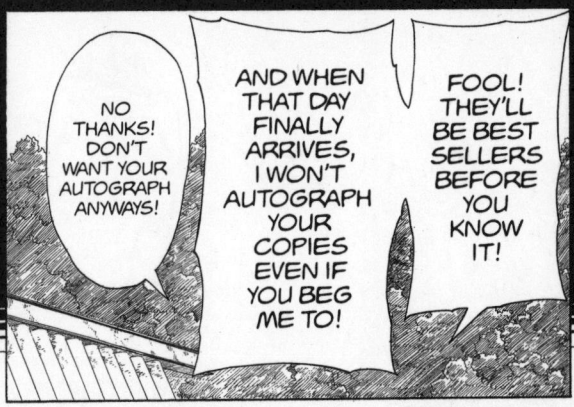
NO THANKS! DON'T WANT YOUR AUTOGRAPH ANYWAYS!
AND WHEN THAT DAY FINALLY ARRIVES, I WON'T AUTOGRAPH YOUR COPIES EVEN IF YOU BEG ME TO!
FOOL! THEY'LL BE BEST SELLERS BEFORE YOU KNOW IT!

...
WITH THOSE BOOKS THAT DON'T SELL?

...CUZ YOU GAVE ME SOME-THING MUCH MORE VALUABLE.

TALES OF A NINJA SHINOBI

ARE YOU ALL RIGHT, SASUKE?
YEAH... LET'S HURRY.
WE'RE ALMOST AT THE RENDEZ-VOUS POINT.
HUF
HUF
WHUMP

I KNEW YOU COULD DO IT.
NICE WORK.

AS PROMISED, I'VE DELIVERED EIGHT TAILS TO YOU.

...TO KONO-HA.

THEN...
FIRST, TO HEAL.

WHERE ARE YOU GOING?

FRRILL

READ THIS WAY
...SO TELL ME THE TRUTH... WHAT ARE YOUR INTENTIONS?
NOW THAT YOU KNOW THE WHOLE TRUTH ABOUT ITACHI AND HIS LIFE...
...THERE IS THE POSSIBILITY THAT YOU WILL TAKE HIS POSITION AND TRY TO PROTECT KONOHA.
SASUKE, I NEED TO ASK YOU SOMETHING IMPORTANT.
I DO NOT WANT PEACE BOUGHT WITH ITACHI'S LIFE.
BUT MY GRIEF AT LOSING HIM IS DEEPER THAN ANY DESIRE TO FOLLOW HIS PATH...
ITACHI'S LIFE SHOWS HOW HE SACRIFICED HIMSELF TO PROTECT THE VILLAGE.
...
...INCON-SOLABLY SO.
AND I BELIEVE THAT EVERYONE IN KONOHA ENJOYING THE PEACE GAINED IN EXCHANGE FOR ITACHI'S LIFE IS GUILTY TOO.
MOST OF ALL, I WILL NEVER FORGIVE THE THREE ELDERS.
NOW THAT I KNOW THE TRUTH, I WILL NEVER TAKE HIS SIDE AND PROTECT KONOHA.
KRAKKA

YOU CAN IGNORE ITACHI'S WILL, HIS SACRIFICE...
ARE YOU SURE?
...THOSE HE STROVE TO PROTECT?
NO... I WANT TO SLAUGHTER ALL OF KONOHA, BUT BY MYSELF...
I THOUGHT YOU WERE ONLY GOING TO KILL THE ELDERS?
...I WAS JUST FEIGNING IN FRONT OF TAKA.
THAT'S ALL.
THEN I FEEL SIMILARLY ...
THAT ITACHI'S LIFE IS MORE PRECIOUS THAN KONOHA...
...WAS BECAUSE MY LIFE WAS MORE PRECIOUS THAN THE VILLAGE...
YOU TOLD ME...
...THE REASON ITACHI COULDN'T KILL ME...
TO ME THEY ARE THE SCUM OF THE EARTH!
BUT ALL THOSE IN KONOHA WHO ABIDE BY SENJU!
AND IT WAS NOT ONLY THE ELDERS WHO CHASED ITACHI TO HIS DEATH...
ORDERED MY BROTHER TO KILL OUR PARENTS!
THEY DISCRIMINATED AGAINST UCHIHA!

READ THIS WAY
IF YOU WANT TO RIDICULE ME AS A BRAT SWAYED BY HIS EMOTIONS, GO AHEAD.
...
THEY ARE ALL OBJECTS OF MY VEN-GEANCE !!
...I'D KILL THEIR LOVED ONES LEFT AND RIGHT!
IF ANYONE WHO WOULD DISPARAGE MY WAY OF LIVING WERE TO COME FORWARD ...
THE FOOLISH SPUTTERING OF THOSE WHO DON'T KNOW HATRED.
TO ACCEPT AND ADOPT ITACHI'S INTENTION WOULD BE CHILDISH.
SO THAT THEY TOO COULD GRASP WHAT IT'S LIKE...

...TO EXPERI-ENCE THIS HATRED OF MINE.
...YOU LEARN WHAT IT IS TO HATE.
ONCE YOU HAVE BEEN HURT...
...
(LIGHTNING)

...MY PARTNER IS TAILING THEM RIGHT NOW.
AND AMONG THEM IS A MEMBER OF KONOHA'S UCHIHA CLAN...

WHAT?! WHAT'S THIS ABOUT KILLER BEE?
SQUI
SQUI

SHABASH
HOW DARE THE AKATSUKI !!

WHAT SAY YOU, LORD RAIKAGE?

JUST YOU WAIT, MY BROTHER!

Number 477: Raikage on the Move!!

WOO...
THWACK
OWWW!
UNNNH.
NOT USING THE TOAD OIL'S A LOT HARDER THAN I EXPECTED ...!
OF COURSE IT IS!
WHAT DID YA EXPECT, EH?
FOCUS!
YER BODY'S STILL SHIFTIN', JUST BARELY.
TMP
REMEM-BER, DON'T MOVE!

ER... I JUST THOUGHT OF THIS, BUT...
NOT E'EN THE SLIGHTEST QUIVER!
WHAT'S THAT?

...

NOT POS-SIBLE.
WHY NOT?

THEN I WON'T HAVE TO LEARN HOW TO TAKE IN NATURE ENERGY WITHOUT IT...
WHY CAN'T I JUST TAKE THE OIL WITH ME AND USE IT WHEN I HAVE TO FIGHT?!

THE OIL'S JUST A TOOL TO HELP YA GET THE HANG OF THINGS.
...I THOUGHT I TOLD YA!

REALLY ?!
GAH!

IT VAPOR-IZES.
OUT OF MOUNT MYOBOKU'S CLIMATE, THIS OIL RAPIDLY EVAPORATES.

JUST COME ALONG!
...DESPITE HOW IT LOOKS, I DID LEARN ALL THE TRICKS TO FOCUSING FROM...
AWW... BUT...
YER POWERS OF CONCEN-TRATION ARE STILL LACKIN', YA AMATEUR!

YES-SIR!!

THIS OUGHTA DO IT...
WHAT IS THIS PLACE?
SPROING

KLOP
K-KLOP

TAK

READ THIS WAY
SPROING
SPROING
FOLLOW ME, NARUTO-BOY!
?!
YA MUST LEARN TO STOP YER MOTION AS AN ANIMAL.
WRRBL
WAAH!
WRRBBL
GAH!
...
...AND MOTION-LESSLY SYNCHRO-NIZE WITH NATURE!
YA NEED TO FIND YER CENTER OF BALANCE...
WAAH!

?!
FRRL

WE'LL HAVE TO WAIT ON YA TAKIN' IN NATURE ENERGY UNTIL YA PERFECT BEING STILL.

PHEW...
PHE...

SHA BAAN

SHUT UP, SUIGETSU!
JUST BE THANKFUL WE DIDN'T LEAVE YOU BEHIND TOO!

WHY'D YOU LEAVE BEHIND MY EXECUTIONER'S BLADE?!

I ENDED UP THAT WAY FROM PROTECTING YOU ALL!
YOU WERE PASSED OUT AS WELL, KARIN!
HOW DARE YOU!

...ANYWAY, ARE WE REALLY GETTING THE BIJU'S POWER, SASUKE?
FINE...

SO QUIT QUARRELING.
WE WERE ALL PROTECTING EACH OTHER... WE'RE LIKE FISH AND WATER, SO CLOSE WE CAN'T DO WITHOUT EACH OTHER.

WHY NOT?
?
BUT WE ACTUALLY NO LONGER NEED TO DEPEND ON SUCH THINGS.
HEH... WHO KNOWS ...

FSH

I HAVE OBTAINED NEW POWERS!... STRONG ENOUGH TO TAKE DOWN KONOHA...

WHAT'S THE MATTER, SASUKE?

...!

KASHINK

READ THIS WAY
SSH...
... NOTHING. IT'S NOTHING.
WHAT IS IT, KARIN?
I SENSE A CHAKRA OUTSIDE...
...IT SEEMS WE'VE BEEN TAILED.
!
GO NOW!

!!

SHKU NK

SPLICH SPLICH

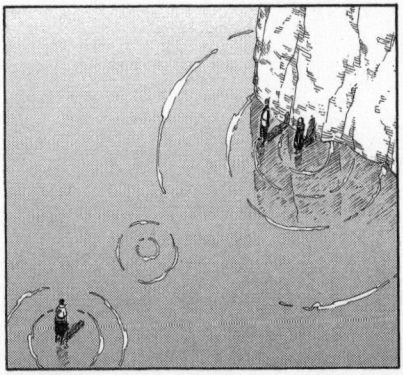

FORGIVE ME, LORD RAIKAGE... IT APPEARS MY TAIL WAS UNSUCCESSFUL.
FSH

ZWOO...
!
IT SEEMS SASUKE WAS SUCCESS-FUL.
ALL THAT'S LEFT IS PAIN.

READ THIS WAY
NOT JUST YUGITO, BUT NOW BEE TOO.
I CAN'T BELIEVE BEE WAS TAKEN DOWN!
WE'VE RECEIVED SEVERAL MESSENGER LIZARDS FROM JAY.
ONCE WE'VE PINPOINTED THE ENEMY'S WHEREABOUTS, WE'LL SEND IN FOUR CELLS...
...RESCUE LORD KILLER BEE, AND WIPE OUT THE ENEMY.
I HEARD A KONOHAGAKURE UCHIHA FELLOW KIDNAPPED MY LITTLE BROTHER!
WHY ARE THERE UCHIHA MEMBERS IN THE AKATSUKI?!
IT WAS UCHIHA SASUKE ...
IT APPEARS HE WENT ROGUE QUITE A WHILE AGO.
WHY ISN'T THE HOKAGE DOING ANYTHING ABOUT THEIR ROGUE NINJA?!
THEY WHO WERE SO QUICK TO REACT OVER THE HYUGA INCIDENT!

雷
SOMETHING'S OFF... THE MESSAGES HAVE CEASED...

NOW WE WILL NO LONGER BE ABLE TO LOCATE THE ENEMY...
IT SEEMS JAY HAS EITHER BEEN KILLED OR CAPTURED.
WHAT ?!!

SEND OUT AN ENTIRE BATTALION IF YOU HAVE TO!
FIGURE OUT AS MUCH AS YOU CAN FROM THE INTEL HE'S ALREADY SENT BACK AND START COMBING THE VICINITY!

I'M GIVING THEM A DOCUMENT OF INTENT TO DELIVER TO KONOHA STATING THAT WE WILL TAKE CARE OF UCHIHA SASUKE!
AND HAVE THEM HAND OVER ALL INTEL ON HIM!
AND SUMMON SAMUI'S CELL!
Y-YES, MILORD.

THE AKATSUKI WILL NOT BE FOR-GIVEN!
FURTHERMORE, I'M GOING TO CONVENE A GOKAGE SUMMIT CONFERENCE! A MEETING OF THE FIVE SHADOWS.

OMOI, KARUI...
...LORD RAIKAGE HAS SUM-MONED US.

COULD HE HAVE FOUND OUT THAT MY BODY MASS INDEX HAS SPIKED?
...OR ARE WE ABOUT TO GET REPRI-MANDED?
WHAT IN THE WORLD COULD IT BE? MAYBE THERE'S A CRISIS ...
WAS IT BECAUSE I PUT MAYONNAISE ON MY POTATOES?

YOU KNOW, BEING AROUND YOU GUYS IS PRETTY TIRING.
MUUNH MUUNH
AAAH, MY SHOULDERS!

OMOI... YOU ALWAYS THINK TOO MUCH!
THE MOST THAT WOULD HAPPEN IS YOU COULD GET SENT TO BUY PROTEIN.
YOU WOULDN'T GET REPRIMANDED FOR SOMETHING SO TRIVIAL!

YOU OUGHT TO THINK THINGS THROUGH MORE CAREFULLY.
QUIT YAKKING AND LET'S GO!
AWW, WILL YOU SHUT UP!
JUST BECAUSE YOU DON'T GET TIGHT SHOULDERS BECAUSE YOU'RE FLAT-CHESTED...

SOMETIMES, TIGHT SHOULDERS ARE ACTUALLY A...
YOUR SHOULDERS ARE PROBABLY SORE BECAUSE OF YOUR WELL-ENDOWED FIGURE... BUT THERE'S A CHANCE IT'S SOMETHING ELSE.

COME ON, THAT'S ENOUGH, YOU TWO.
LET'S GO!
...THAT KICK'S JUST THE BEG—
OWW!
THOK
SHUT UP!!

ZWOO...

Number 418: Sage Naruto!!

IT'S GOIN' WELL.

ZWOO...

ZWOOO...

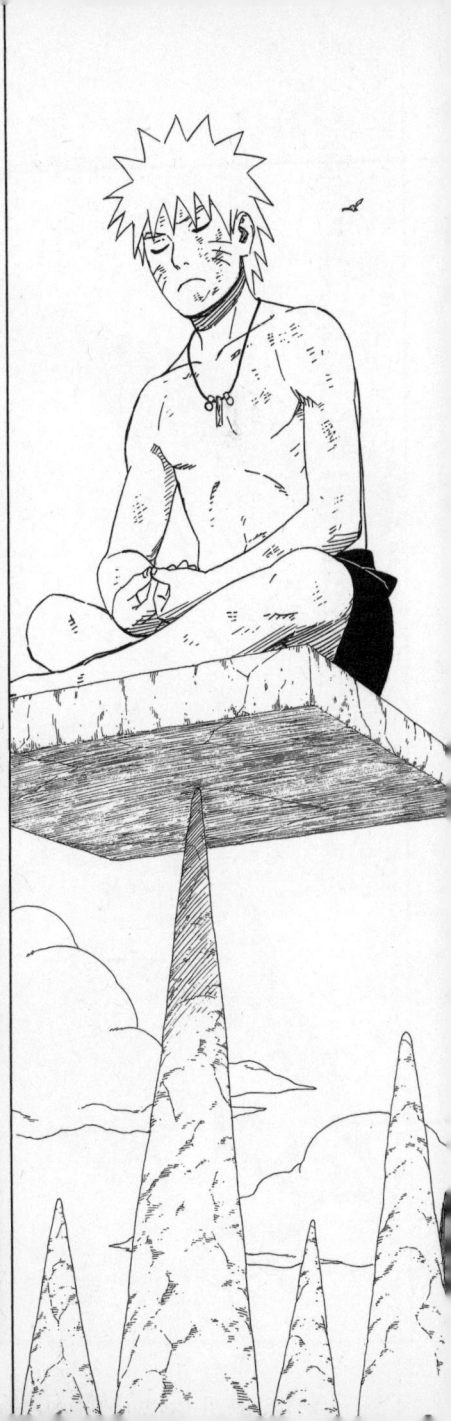

READ THIS WAY
ZWOOOOO...
...I REALLY AM IMPRESSED HOW FAR HE'S GOTTEN WITHOUT USING THE OIL...
HE'S FINALLY GOT IT...

RI
NG

WELL, HOW DOES IT FEEL?
IT SEEMS HE'S ABLE TO BUILD UP EVEN MORE SAGE JUTSU CHAKRA THAN WHEN HE WAS USIN' THE OIL TOO.

AND NO FROG ASPECTS EITHER! THIS MIGHT MEAN NARUTO-BOY HAS BECOME A SAGE EXCEEDIN' JIRAIYA-BOY!
HE'S DISPLAYIN' THE RINGS AROUND THE EYES— PROOF OF SUCCESSFUL SAGEHOOD!

!
TAK

FRRLLP FRRLLP

I KINDA GET NOW WHAT IT MEANS TO BECOME ONE WITH NATURE...
YEAH...

...

VWIIT...
WAAH!

ZWUMP
WAAAAAH!!
THOOM
IT DOESN'T HURT THAT MUCH...
FSH
OW... HUH?
OWWW ...
KATOK KATOK KATOK

W-WOW ...
SAGE MODE, HUH.

YER WHOLE BODY BECOMES ACTIVATED IN ALL DIFFER-ENT WAYS.
AND THAT IS SAGE MODE.
TMP

NOW THAT YOU'VE MASTERED SAGE MODE TOO, WE GOT ONE FINAL STEP LEFT.
WHAT?! ONE FINAL STEP...
YOU MEAN WE'RE NOT DONE YET?!

IT'S A TYPE O' SPARRING THAT SAGES PERFORM USIN' SAGE JUTSU CHAKRA.
NOW I SHALL TEACH YOU HOW TO DO KAWAZU KUMITE, TO SPAR WITH FROGS!

SPLISH
SPLISH
SPLISH
SPLISH
UNF
KABOOM
THOK
THOK

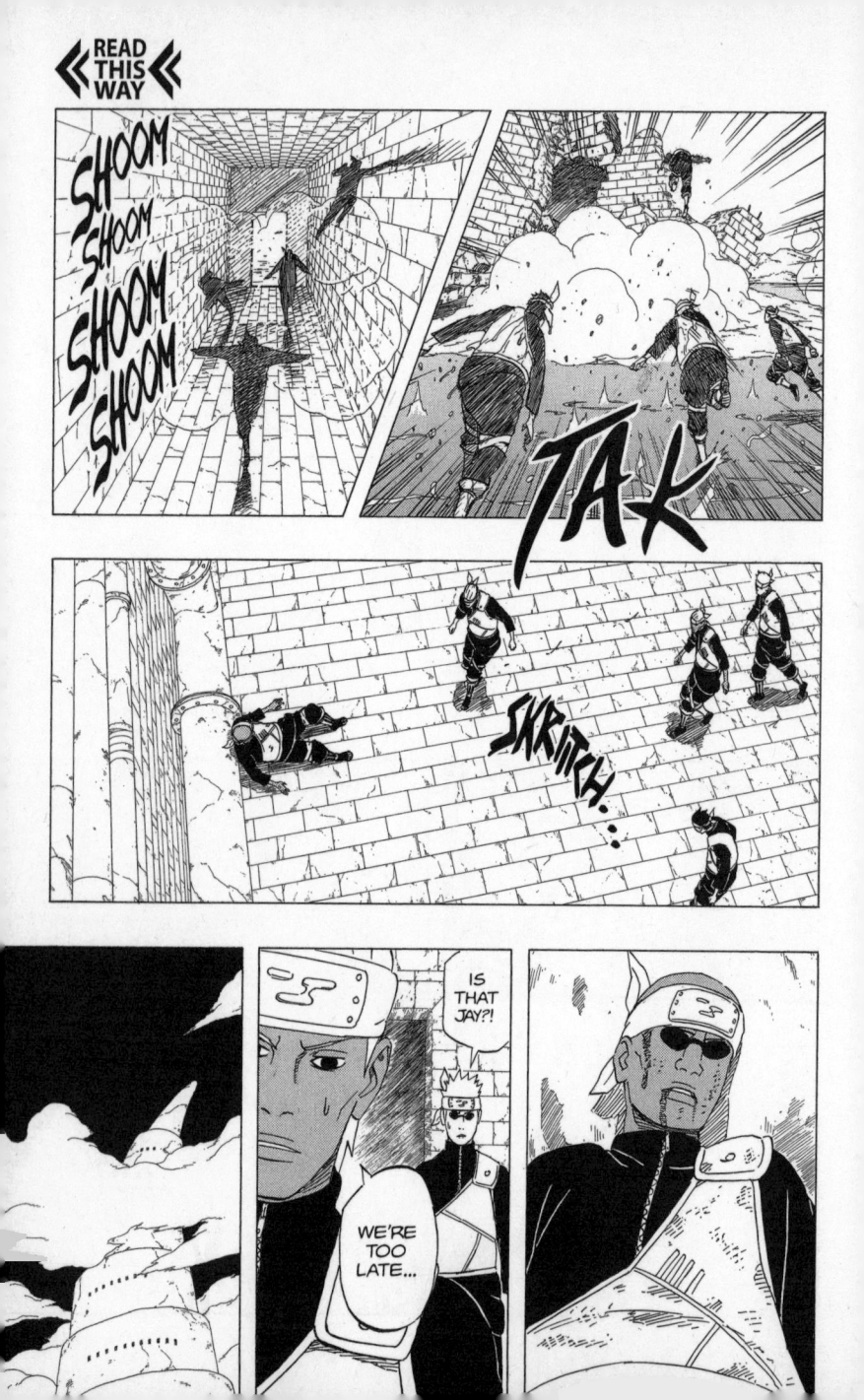
READ THIS WAY
SHOOM SHOOM SHOOM SHOOM
TAK
SKRITCH...
IS THAT JAY?!
WE'RE TOO LATE...

SWOOO...

I MUST TRY IT IN SAGE MODE...

FSSSH FSSSH

HUF

FWOO...

...EVEN THOUGH IT'S STILL FAR FROM PERFECT...

I DID IT!

SNNZZZZ

SNNZZZZ

...AND MAKE SURE NO ONE CATCHES ME.

(CIPHER CORPS)

(KONOHAGAKURE INTEL DIVISION)

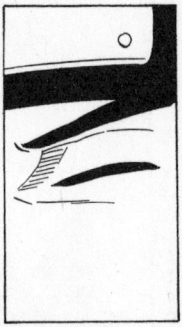

I SUSPECT IT'S SOME JUTSU OF PAIN'S OR SOME-THING.
BE CAREFUL. THERE MAY BE GENJUTSU TRAPS SET IN THERE AS WELL.

IT'S NO USE... SOMEONE'S PLACED BLOCKS INSIDE HIS MIND.
IT'S GO-ING TO BE DIFFICULT TO NAVIGATE PAST THEM.

ZWOOO

I KNOW.

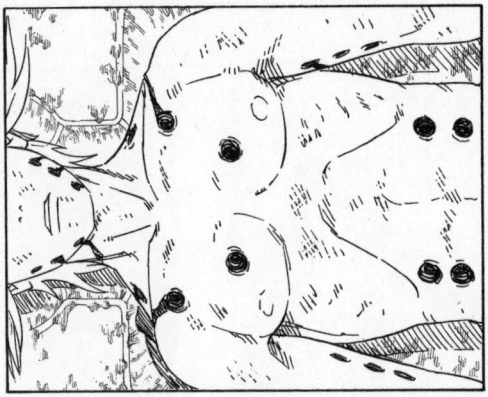

(AUTOPSY ROOM 3)

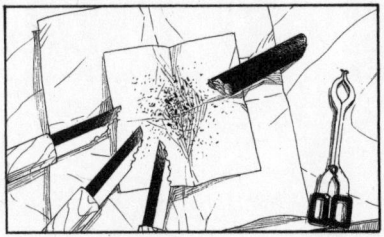

TMP TMP TMP TMP
TMP TMP

NOW IS THE TIME TO DELIVER PAIN TO THE WORLD...

NARUTO

Number 419: Raid!!

KONAN, YOU'RE WITH THE HUNT.
I KNOW.
SH
KE
EN
KONOHA IS PROTECTED BY A SPHERICAL BARRIER THAT ENCOMPASSES BOTH THE VILLAGE ITSELF AND THE AIR ABOVE IT.
IT IS SET UP SO THAT ANYONE WHO TRIES TO ENTER WITHOUT PERMISSION IS DETECTED IMMEDI-ATELY.

READ THIS WAY
HOW DID ITACHI AND KISAME ENTER AND LEAVE SO EASILY...?
SHUP
HE KNEW THE JUTSU CODE TO GET THROUGH THE BARRIER.
ITACHI WAS ONCE KONOHA BLACK OPS.
AS EXPLAINED, WE WILL LAUNCH CHIKUSHODO INTO THE SKIES ABOVE THE VILLAGE– AFTER INFILTRATING THE BARRIER SHE WILL SUMMON US.
WAIT FOR CHIKU-SHODO'S SUMMON-ING.
WE WILL CONFUSE THE ENEMY BY NOT GIVING THEM AN ACCURATE COUNT.
FWITAP
I HAVE MY OWN WAY OF DOING THINGS.
FW
P
FRR
LL

FITIK
!

PHOOM

FIDOLP...
INTRU-DER!

FSH

SINGLE TARGET, WEST GATE, SECTOR I-B.
!

TMP
B-B-
BOOF
SHOOM
DIS-PERSE !!
...
ZW
OOP
SKRIITCH

WHAT'S THAT?
KABOOSH
BA-ROOMBLE
BA-ROOMBLE
KER
BOOSH
ARGH!

BO
OF
WAAAH!!
WHAT THE?!
THOM
AND NOTIFY THE HOKAGE AS WELL! STAT!!
GAH! THIS IS BEYOND THE SCOPE OF JUST THE DEFENSE SHIELD CELL!
CONTACT OTHER TROOPS AND REQUEST BACKUP!
SIMUL-TANEOUS ATTACKS!
WHAT'S GOING ON?! I THOUGHT THERE WAS ONLY ONE INTRUDER!
I'LL CONFIRM WITH THE BYAKUGAN RIGHT AWAY!!

NO INFOR-MATION ON NINE TAILS, EH...
KKRNNKH

THOMP

ZWOP

(FROM RAIKAGE)

JUST CUZ I'M WORRIED DOESN'T MEAN I'M GOING TO RUSH TO CRAZY CONCLUSIONS!
AREN'T YOU WORRIED ABOUT LORD BEE?!

HE'S OUR TEACHER! THE LORD KILLER BEE!
SHUT UP!! I JUST DON'T WANT TO HEAR YOUR PESSIMISTIC THEORIES!
THERE'S NO WAY HE'D GET DEFEATED !!

雷
FSSSSH...
WE SHALL RESCUE BEE NO MATTER WHAT IT TAKES!!
WE WILL RESCUE HIM!!

STOP IT, YOU TWO...!
!

ZWOOO...

LORD RAIKAGE ...!!
FSSSSH
FSSSSH

READ THIS WAY
ZWOOOOO...
SHUT UP AND FOCUS!
WITH SO FEW PEOPLE, IT SURE IS TAKING A WHILE.
?!
BOOF

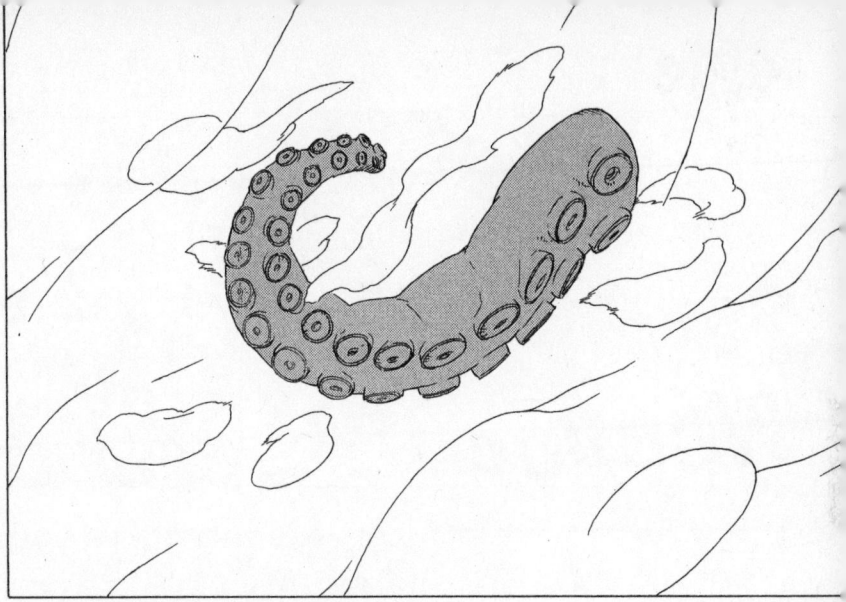

SPLAT

IT APPEARS... SASUKE HAS BLUNDERED ...
SWSH...

TKIK
TKIK

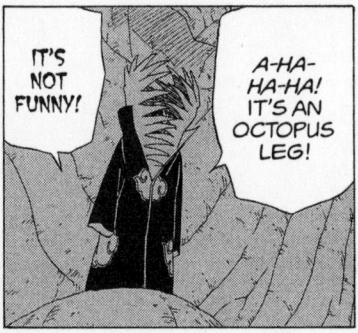
IT'S NOT FUNNY!
A-HA-HA-HA! IT'S AN OCTOPUS LEG!

...

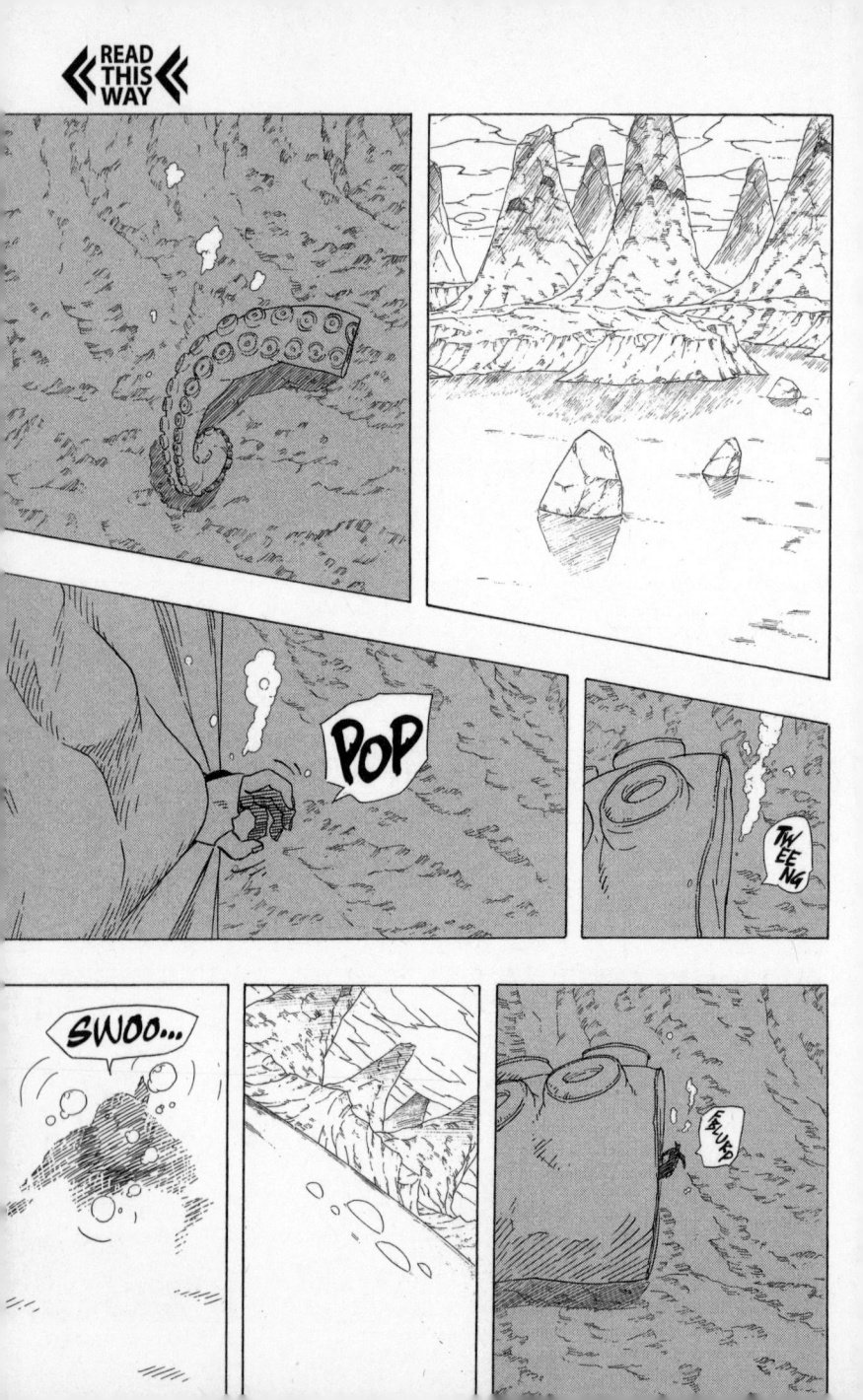
READ THIS WAY
POP
THEENG
SWOO...
EBUSS

SPLASH

I CAME UP WITH IT ON THE SPUR OF THE MOMENT AND IT ENDED UP BEING A GRAND SCHEME.
SUUUAASH

SPRRSH

VWEENT
VWEENT
GOOD... THERE'S NO ONE NEARBY.

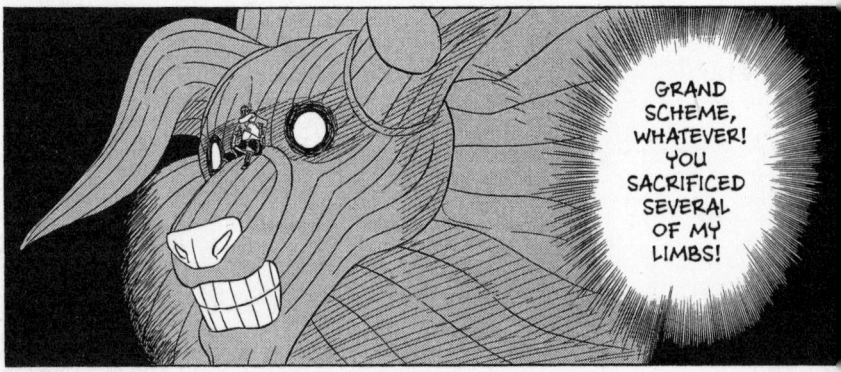
GRAND SCHEME, WHATEVER! YOU SACRIFICED SEVERAL OF MY LIMBS!

WILL YOU QUIT SPEAKING TO ME IN THAT ANNOYING RAP?! YOU NINCOM-POOP!!

NOW, NOW, DON'T GET MAD, MY BOY EIGHT-O ♪ YA KNOW THEY'LL REGROW ♪ AND YA KNOW I WAS RIGHT, YO.
!!

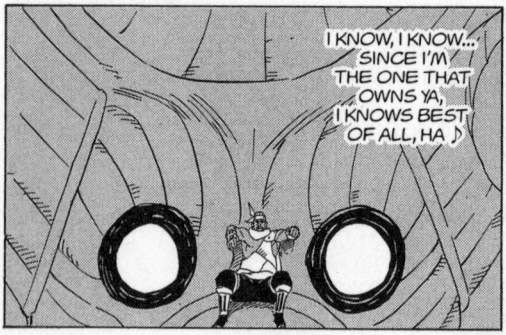
I KNOW, I KNOW... SINCE I'M THE ONE THAT OWNS YA, I KNOWS BEST OF ALL, HA ♪

SLOSH
SLOSH

SO THIS TIME, I THINK I'LL TRY...

YOU'LL TRY WHAT? ANOTHER HALF-CRACKED IDEA?! DON'T YOU DO IT!

YEA!!
ENKA ...!
...

ARE YOU SURE THIS IS A GOOD IDEA?
I BET RAIKAGE IS ON THE RAMPAGE RIGHT NOW...

SINCE EVERYONE THINKS I'M STILL IN THE AKATSUKI'S GRASP.
STILL, NOW I CAN FINALLY ESCAPE BROTHER'S MEDDLESOME SNOOPIN' AND GET OUT OF THE VILLAGE. FREEDOM, MAN!

SO... WHAT ARE YOU PLANNING TO DO?

I NEED A BREATHER EVERY ONCE IN A WHILE, YOU KNOW.
WELL, I HAVE BEEN IMPRISONED AS A WEAPON IN THIS VILLAGE BECAUSE I'M A JINCHŪ-RIKI...

PLUS, HAVING SUMMONED ME, YOU DON'T HAVE MUCH STAMINA LEFT.
DID YOU REALLY NEED TO CALL ON ME WHEN YOU HAD THE UPPER HAND?
HOW CAN YOU BE SO FLIPPANT... THE AKATSUKI WON'T SIT STILL THAT LONG.

WHO'S THAT?
WHEN IT COMES TO ENKA, MASTER SABU-CHAN'S DA MAN!
BLAZE DA NAME INTO YA BRAIN, FOOL. HE'S DA KING OF ENKA NINJA.

HUH? THROUGH MY ENKA?
...TIMES MAY BE A-CHANGING SOON...

I GOT CARRIED AWAY.
WELL, THAT SHARINGAN DUDE'S PROBABLY THE TOUGHEST FELLOW I'VE EVER FOUGHT...
SHUPSHUP

YER KAWAZU KUMITE IS GOIN' QUITE WELL TOO.
IMPRESSIVE JUMPIN' ABILITY!
TMP
KASH
KASH
KASH
KASH
KASH
Number 420: Battlefield Konoha!!
BO
HEH!
ART OF THE SHADOW DOPPEL-GANGER !!!
OF
TA
K
TMP

READ THIS WAY
TMP
AND THAT WAS JUST A WARM-UP!!
UNH ...
ARE YOU ALL RIGHT ?!
KSH
!
FSH

Number 420: Battlefield, Konoha!!

NARUTO

READ THIS WAY
...HUH... SO HE'S AKATSUKI...
TELL ME THE LOCATION OF NINE TAILS' JINCHŪRIKI HOST.
SSSH...
OR I SHALL DESTROY YOU.
SPEAK NOW.
I HAVE NO INTENTION OF TELLING YOU ANYTHING.
SU
I SEE...

FW!
TAP
...WHILE THE OTHER HALF HUNTS IN THE SHADOWS ...
ONE HALF LOUDLY WREAKING HAVOC TO DIVERT OUR ATTENTION ...

KAKA-SHI!
THUP

GOOD LUCK, KAKASHI.

FWIP
ROGER!

LEAVE THIS SCENE TO ME.
TAKE THAT INJURED FELLOW WITH YOU AND WITH-DRAW.

TAK

EARTH STYLE! MUD WALL !!
WHUMP
HFF
SH
SH
D-D-D-D-DOOM
UGH!
SH
NCK
FSH

TA
LIGHT-NING BLADE!!
K
BZZAR
BZZAK
!
WHAT WAS THAT?

THE MIRROR NINJA HATAKE KAKASHI... IT IS AN HONOR TO MEET YOU.
TELL ME, WHERE IS NINE TAILS?
SQUILCH
THAT'S A SILLY QUESTION.
TAK
BZZZ
ZAKK
ARGH!
TOK

ALL RIGHT, I'M GONNA PROCURE US SOME FRESH INGREDI-ENTS.

NNGRG

MA, GET SOME STAMINA-BUILDIN' STUFF, EH!
NOT GROSS STUFF AGAIN... UGH...

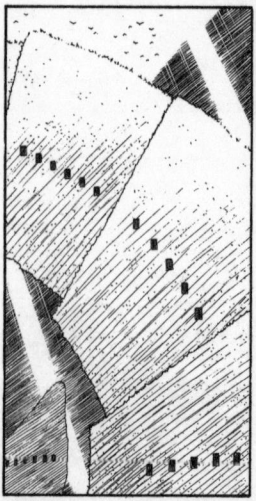

WH-WHAT'S THAT?
YOU'RE SUDDENLY SO SERIOUS.

NOW THAT YOU'RE NOT ONLY ABLE TO MANIPULATE SAGE JUTSU CHAKRA...
...BUT HAVE MASTERED THE BASICS OF KAWAZU KUMITE AND SAGE TECHNIQUES ...
...I NEED TO DISCUSS WIT' YA ONE FINAL THING.

WELL ...
...IT'S ABOUT THE RISKS OF USIN' THE SAGE MODE.

THAT'S RIGHT...
...ONCE YA FULLY GRASP THESE HERE RISKS...
...YA CAN EXPLOIT SAGE MODE TO ITS FULLEST EXTENT!

RISKS ...?

AND TO ENTER SAGE MODE, YA GOTTA DRAW IN NATURE ENERGY, FOR WHICH YA NEED TO FOLLOW THE PRINCIPLE DON'T MOVE.
WHICH MEANS YA CAN'T USE IT WHEN YER ALREADY IN THE MIDST OF BATTLE.
FOR IF YA STOP MOVIN', YA BECOME AN EASY TARGET FOR YER ENEMY.

WHAT RISKS?
FIRST, AS YA'VE PROBABLY ALREADY FIGGERED OUT, YA CAN'T MAINTAIN SAGE MODE FOR TOO LONG... MAYBE FIVE MINUTES AT MOST.

READ THIS WAY
SO WHAT WAS ALL THIS TRAINING FOR...?!
WHA ?!!
THAT'S STUPID!
IF YA EVER HAVE TO GO INTO SAGE MODE WHEN YER BY YERSELF...
...YA GOTTA WITHDRAW FROM THE BATTLE IN ORDER TO GATHER NATURE ENERGY.
SO THE ONLY TIME YA CAN GO INTO SAGE MODE IS WHEN YA GOT PLENTY OF COMRADES AROUND YA THAT CAN FREE YA UP.
IF YOU AND I MERGE OUR BODIES, IT'LL BE FINE!
WHAT DO YOU MEAN ?
THAT'S WHAT I'M HERE FOR.
DON'T BE SO GLUM.
KB-BIT-KB-BIT-KB-BIT
KB-KB-BIT
...

AAAARGH!!!
ALL IT MEANS IS I'LL BE LOOSELY ATTACHED TO YER SHOULDER OR BACK.

TO PUT IT SIMPLY, IT MEANS TO SPLIT THE ROLES OF STILLNESS AND ACTION.
WHILE ONE OF US IS MOVIN', THE OTHER IS BEIN' STILL 'N TAKIN' IN NATURE ENERGY.

O-OHHH.
BUT WHY IS IT GONNA BE FINE IF WE DO THIS MERGE THING?

OKAY... I GET IT NOW.

IN JIRAIYA-BOY'S CASE, THE FINAL FORM OF HIS SAGE MODE HAD MA AND ME BOTH RIDIN' HIS SHOULDERS.
油

TA
K
ALL RIGHT !!

FSH
DON'T YA WORRY, NARUTO-BOY!

検死室 3
担当
シズネ
オヨネ
クマドリ

WHICH MEANS ?
DE... MODU-LATORS ...?

BUT THESE ARE DEMODU-LATORS THAT RESPOND TO HIGH-FREQUENCY CHAKRA WAVES.
THE CHAKRA METER SUD-DENLY REACTED AND THESE BLACK RODS STARTED EMITTING HEAT, WHICH I THOUGHT WAS WEIRD.

IN SHORT, THEY'RE CHAKRA RECEIVERS!
AND IT'S RECEIVING CHAKRA NOW!

THE FACT THAT THEY ARE RECEIV-ERS...
...NEVER MIND THAT... I MUST REPORT THIS TO LADY TSUNADE RIGHT AWAY!

WHAT DO YOU MEAN?
...RECEIV-ERS?

WHAT THE?!
THOOOM...
!
!

SUP
FRRRRR

木ノ葉隠れ情報

LET'S GO!
WHAT'S THAT...?

!
SHK

CL
O
P
WHUMM

FOUND IT.

SHK
SHKSHKSHK

WHOOSH
BAROOMBLE
WHAT?
!
BAROOMBLE
!
?!

TMP

?!

FATHER! THE VILLAGE, IT'S...!

IT'S FINALLY HAPPENED...

油
FOR JIRAIYA-BOY CLEARLY BEQUEATHED HIS ALL TO HIM.
IT MAKES ME HOPE MORE THAN ANYTHIN'... THAT HE IS THE CHILD O' PROPHECY.

AND...
SOUND THE STATE OF EMER-GENCY ALARM.

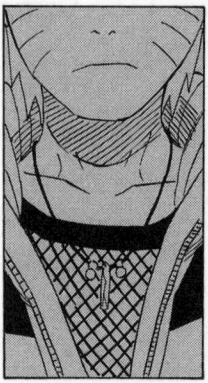

... RECALL NARUTO!

NARUTO

AIEE!
RUN!
HEY, DON'T PUSH!
HURRY!
Number 421: Recall Naruto!!
BOOM
あめ
AIEE!
THWUMP
RUN!!
TAMI!
SWOOO
ZWOOOO

Number 421: Recall Naruto!!

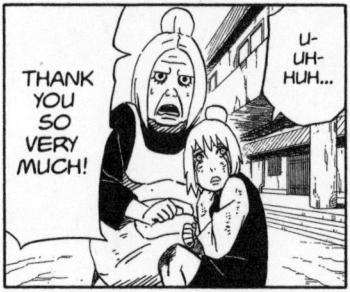

SAKURA!
!
TMP

THANK YOU...
FWOO
OH, GOOD! THIS WOUND'S NOT TOO BAD.

THE AKATSUKI ...
WHAT'S GOING ON?
...IS ATTACKING KONOHA! THEY WANT NARUTO!

ARE YOU ALL RIGHT?
MAS-TER IRUKA ...
SHUP

I CAN'T BELIEVE THEY'D ATTACK US DIRECTLY...

THE ALARM SHOULD SOUND SOON.
I'VE ALREADY ALERTED LADY TSUNADE.

THE AKA-TSUKI ?!

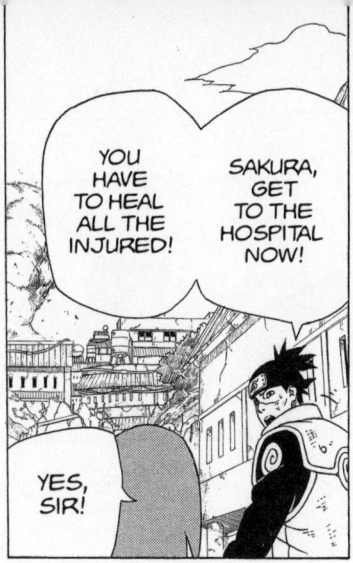
YOU HAVE TO HEAL ALL THE INJURED!
SAKURA, GET TO THE HOSPITAL NOW!
YES, SIR!

KA BOOM
LET'S GO, IRUKA!
!
!
AIEE!

ROGER!
I'M OFF TO GET NARUTO!

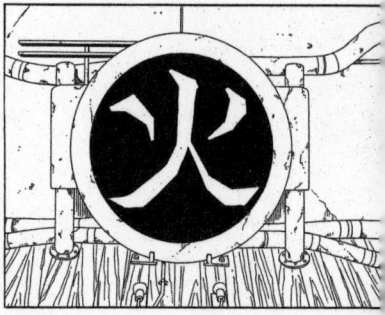
火

SHUP
NO.
LEAVE HIM AT MOUNT MYOBOKU.

I'M COUNT-ING ON YOU!

!
FSH
FSH
FSH

ACCORDING TO DANZO'S REPORT...
...OUR ATTACKER IS THE AKATSUKI LEADER.
AND HE'S AFTER NARUTO, THE JINCHÛ-RIKI.

WHAT ?!

KLOP
KLOP
IF NARUTO IS TAKEN DOWN AND NINE TAILS FALLS INTO THEIR HANDS...

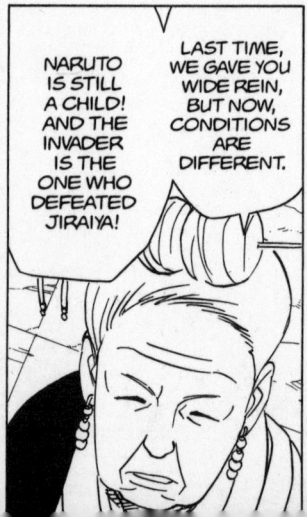
LAST TIME, WE GAVE YOU WIDE REIN, BUT NOW, CONDITIONS ARE DIFFERENT.
NARUTO IS STILL A CHILD! AND THE INVADER IS THE ONE WHO DEFEATED JIRAIYA!

SO?

FWOP
UGH ...!
WHA?! ...WHAT ARE YOU DOING?!

UNTIL I BECOME HOKAGE, THERE'S NO WAY I'M GONNA DIE!!

I CAN'T SIT AROUND DOING NOTHING!

I WILL AVENGE PERVY SAGE!

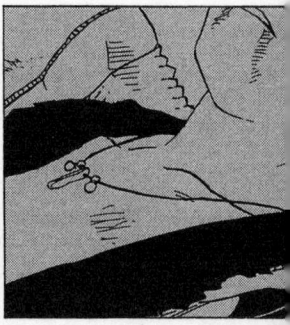

OUR JOB IS TO SET EXAMPLES FOR AND AID THE NEXT GENERATION.
FOR THAT CAUSE, I'LL GLADLY RISK MY LIFE.

I CAN 'SEE THAT THAT CHILD TRULY LOVED 'N ADMIRED JIRAIYA-BOY.
IT MAKES ME HOPE MORE THAN ANY-THIN'... THAT HE IS THE CHILD O' PROPH-ECY.

H-HEY! LET US GO, TSUNADE ...!
HOW DARE YOU RAISE YOUR HAND AGAINST US COUNSELORS ...
WHAT ARE YOU THINKING?!

FOR JIRAIYA-BOY CLEARLY BEQUEATHED HIS ALL TO HIM.

WHAT ARE YOU THINKING ?!
STILL TREATING HIM LIKE A MERE CHILD !!

HE'S ADOPTED THE KONOHA WILL OF FIRE!
HE'S GROWN.
NARUTO IS CURRENTLY TRAINING TO SURPASS JIRAIYA!!

WHA ...?!

HE IS NOT A BACK-UP WEAPON TO BE HIDDEN AWAY!
HE IS UZUMAKI NARUTO, TRUE SHINOBI AND DEFENDER OF KONOHA!

...DO YOU KNOW WHAT JIRAIYA, MASTER SARUTOBI, AND EVEN GRANNY CHIYO OF THE SAND HAD...
...THAT YOU LACK?!

WHA!
UGH...
THUMP
FFT
FFT
THUMP

...

...

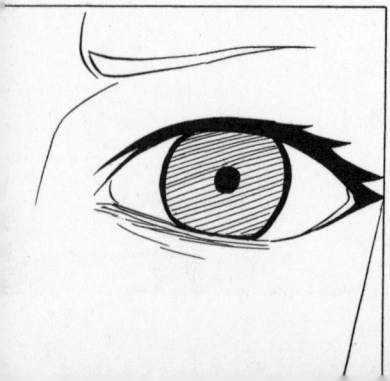

FAITH AND TRUST !!

医
JUST AS MY GRAND-FATHER THE FIRST HOKAGE BELIEVED IN YOU AND ENTRUSTED KONOHA TO YOU...
...IT IS NOW YOUR TURN TO DO THE SAME FOR THE CURRENT YOUTH OF KONOHA!!

SSH...
SSH...

...
...

...DO AS YOU PLEASE...

SH UP

HAVE YOU DISCOVERED SOMETHING?
SHI-ZUNE!

!
LADY TSUNADE!

READ THIS WAY
KA TOK...
WHAT WAS THAT JUTSU?
KA TOK KA TOK...
THERE'S DEFINITELY A BLAST AREA WITH HIM AT THE EPI-CENTER.
IT FELT DIF-FERENT FROM A BLAST WAVE... BUT WHAT COULD IT BE?!
KA TOK...
RIZZZZZAP
HMM... HOW ABOUT THIS?
RIZZZAP

ZZZ
DM

SWSH

IMPRES-SIVE... SO HOW SHALL...
HE CAN REPEL BOTH PHYSICAL ATTACKS AND NINJUTSU, EH...

AN-OTHER ONE...

THO
OM

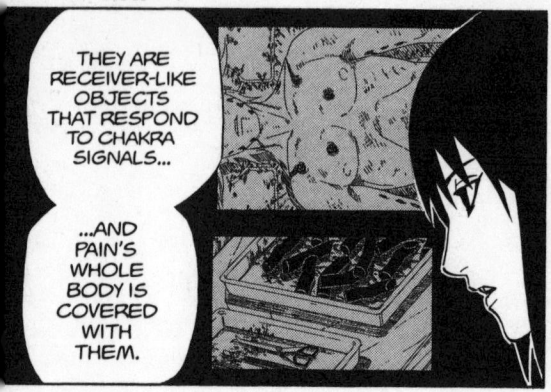
THEY ARE RECEIVER-LIKE OBJECTS THAT RESPOND TO CHAKRA SIGNALS...
...AND PAIN'S WHOLE BODY IS COVERED WITH THEM.

THIS IS IT!

...RECEIVERS, HUH? OR PERHAPS THEY'RE SOME SORT OF WIRELESS RADIO SO THEY CAN COMMUNICATE WITH EACH OTHER USING THEIR CHAKRA...
AND THIS THING IS STILL REACTING, EVEN NOW...

DO YOU MEAN, TO COORDINATE THEIR MOVEMENTS, THEY RECEIVE SOME CHAKRA SIGNAL ACROSS THEIR ENTIRE BODIES?
ACCORDING TO LORD FUKASAKU, ALL SIX PAINS HAD SIMILAR OBJECTS STUDDING THEIR BODIES AND FACES.

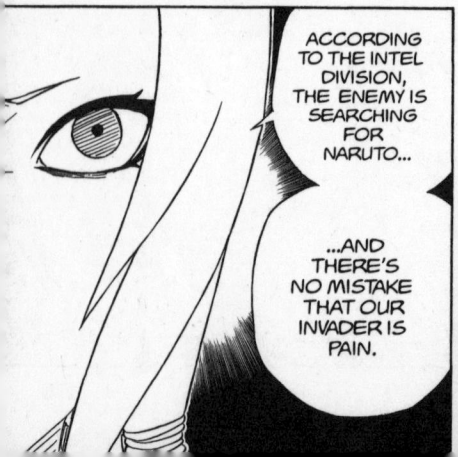
ACCORDING TO THE INTEL DIVISION, THE ENEMY IS SEARCHING FOR NARUTO...
...AND THERE'S NO MISTAKE THAT OUR INVADER IS PAIN.

TO CLARIFY, I WILL COMPARE THIS TO THE DATA FROM THE INTERROGATION CORPS!
THIS HAS TO BE THE KEY TO THE SECRET OF PAIN'S STRENGTH!

SURE THING!

MESSENGER FROG, DON'T JUST RECALL NARUTO—YOU NEED TO PASS THIS INTEL ALONG AS WELL!
WE SHOULD RELAY ALL OF THIS TO LORD FUKASAKU AS WELL.

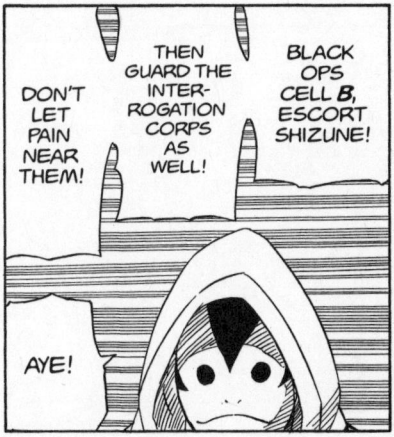
DON'T LET PAIN NEAR THEM!
THEN GUARD THE INTER-ROGATION CORPS AS WELL!
BLACK OPS CELL B, ESCORT SHIZUNE!
AYE!

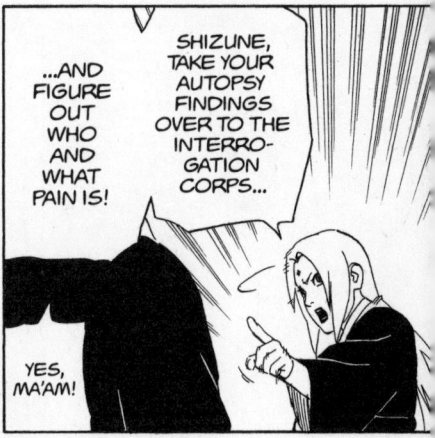
...AND FIGURE OUT WHO AND WHAT PAIN IS!
SHIZUNE, TAKE YOUR AUTOPSY FINDINGS OVER TO THE INTERRO-GATION CORPS...
YES, MA'AM!

LET'S GO!!

I SHALL DEFEND THE VILLAGE WITH ALL MY POWER!
IN THE MEANTIME, AS I AWAIT MORE REPORTS FROM THE ROOF AND HEAL THE INJURED THROUGH KATSUYU...

READ THIS WAY
THWUMP
TAKK
SPRRCHT
OKAY! TIME FOR ME TO GET GOIN' TO LORD FUKASAKU!
FWP
NOW, NINE TAILS CAN BE KEPT CAGED UP.

NARUTO

Number 422: Kakashi vs. Pain!!

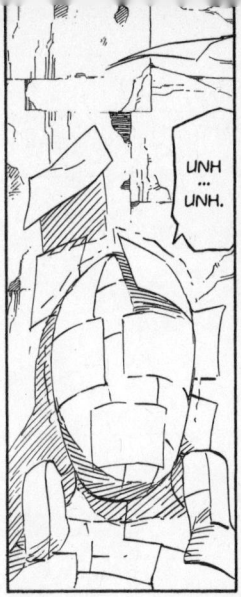
UNH ... UNH.

GRRRR
GRRRR
GRRRR
GRRRR

HUF
HUF
WHERE IS UZUMAKI NARUTO?

PRIIP PRIIP

GRRRR
PRIIP
HUF

DIE ...!

HUF
HUF

WOOOOO...
VW
OOSH

ATTACK HIM DIRECTLY ...
HE... ABSORBS JUTSU...

IS UZUMAKI NARUTO HERE OR NOT?
TELL ME!

UNH ...

王
UGH... I... DON'T KNOW.

BOOF
ART OF SUM-MONING!!
TAK

VERY WELL.
MOUND
MOUND
MOUND
SLINK
SLINK
SLINK
THE VILLAGE IS IN DANGER...
JUST GO!
GO ATTEND TO ALL KONOHA RESIDENTS, BOTH SHINOBI AND NON!
TAKE MY CHAKRA AND HEAL THE INJURED!

I WILL PROTECT THIS VILLAGE...
SPLCH SPLCH SPLCH SPLCH
CRICH CRICH CRICH CRICH
...I SWEAR UPON MY TITLE OF HOKAGE!

BO OM

TMP
!
!
TMP
OVER THERE...!
!
TMP

LET'S GO!

READ THIS WAY
GOT HIM!
FT
AP
WHOOSH
FWMP
THEY SHARE WHAT THEY SEE WITH THE OTHERS.
THEIR VISION IS LINKED!
HE WASN'T EVEN FACING ME...!

JUMP

EACH POSSESSES ONLY A SINGLE JUTSU TYPE... YOU MUST DEDUCE EACH ONE'S ABILITY.
WHEN YOU FACE PAIN, YOU MUST ONLY FIGHT THEM ONE-ON-ONE.

SKRITCH...

!

KRINICH

...THAT'S CRAZY...!
I CAN'T BELIEVE LORD JIRAIYA TOOK ON SIX OF THEM AT ONCE...

READ THIS WAY
KRIK
KRIK
ZWOO...
ZWOO...

FZZMP
?!

FSH

I'M BEING PULLED ...!
THNK

WOOSH

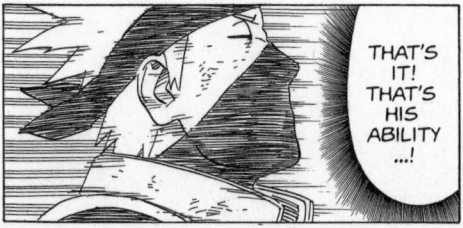
THAT'S IT! THAT'S HIS ABILITY ...!

READ THIS WAY
FRRL
WH-TISH
KRNCH
HAVE TO HOLD THEM OFF AS LONG AS I...
I NEED BACKUP... AND TO LET THE OTHERS KNOW WHAT THE ABILITIES OF THESE TWO ARE!
PAIN... I'VE GOT NO CHANCE IF I FIGHT THEM ALONE.
JNNK
SKRITCH...
GAH...
UGH ...!
THWAP
SHEEN

DUNF

READ THIS WAY
!
BZZZ
BZP
BZP
BZZZ

FWOOM
TAK

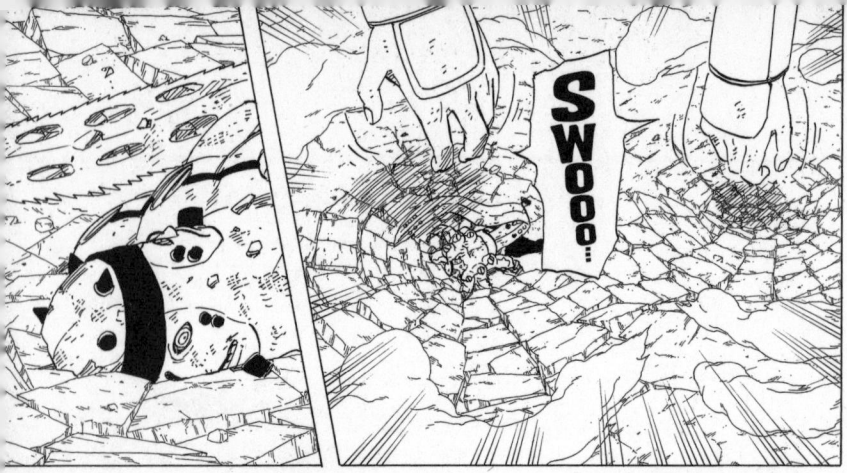

TO BE CONTINUED IN *NARUTO* VOLUME 46!

IN THE NEXT VOLUME...

KNOW THY PAIN

The determination of Naruto and his comrades is tested beyond measure when Kakashi is injured and an attempt to overthrow Tsunade begins. Naruto's friends must fight or fall as Pain commences the final destruction of Konoha. Is the fate of Naruto's beloved village—and that of everyone he loves—finally truly sealed?

AVAILABLE NOW!

THE BEST SELLING MANGA SERIES IN THE WORLD!

ONE PIECE

Story & Art by EIICHIRO ODA

As a child, **Monkey D. Luffy** was inspired to become a pirate by listening to the tales of the buccaneer "Red-Haired" Shanks. But Luffy's life changed when he accidentally ate the Gum-Gum Devil Fruit and gained the power to stretch like rubber...at the cost of never being able to swim again! Years later, still vowing to become the king of the pirates, Luffy sets out on his adventure in search of the legendary "One Piece," said to be the greatest treasure in the world...

ONE PIECE © 1997 by Eiichiro Oda/SHUEISHA Inc.

www.shonenjump.com www.viz.com

You're Reading in the Wrong Direction!!

Whoops! Guess what? You're starting at the wrong end of the comic!

...It's true! In keeping with the original Japanese format, Naruto is meant to be read from right to left, starting in the upper-right corner.

Unlike English, which is read from left to right, Japanese is read from right to left, meaning that action, sound effects and word-balloon order are completely reversed... something which can make readers unfamiliar with Japanese feel pretty backwards themselves. For this reason, manga or Japanese comics published in the U.S. in English have sometimes been published "flopped"—that is, printed in exact reverse order, as though seen from the other side of a mirror.

By flopping pages, U.S. publishers can avoid confusing readers, but the compromise is not without its downside. For one thing, a character in a flopped manga series who once wore in the original Japanese version a T-shirt emblazoned with "M A Y" (as in "the merry month of") now wears one which reads "Y A M"! Additionally, many manga creators in Japan are themselves unhappy with the process, as some feel the mirror-imaging of their art alters their original intentions.

We are proud to bring you Masashi Kishimoto's Naruto in the original unflopped format. For now, though, turn to the other side of the book and let the ninjutsu begin...!

—Editor

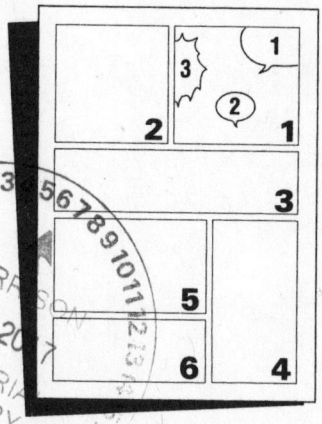

9/17
HARRISON
SEP 2017
MEMORIAL
LIBRARY